# Backyard Animals
# Black Widow Spiders

## Megan Kopp

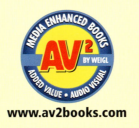

www.av2books.com

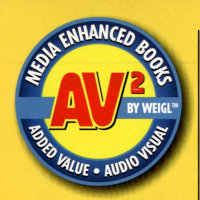

MEDIA ENHANCED BOOKS
AV²
BY WEIGL™
ADDED VALUE • AUDIO VISUAL

AV² provides enriched content that supplements and complements this book. Weigl's AV² books strive to create inspired learning and engage young minds in a total learning experience.

## Your AV² Media Enhanced books come alive with...

### Audio
Listen to sections of the book read aloud.

### Key Words
Study vocabulary, and complete a matching word activity.

### Video
Watch informative video clips.

### Quizzes
Test your knowledge.

### Embedded Weblinks
Gain additional information for research.

### Slide Show
View images and captions, and prepare a presentation.

### Try This!
Complete activities and hands-on experiments.

### ... and much, much more!

Go to **www.av2books.com,** and enter this book's unique code.

## BOOK CODE

U655752

**AV² by Weigl** brings you media enhanced books that support active learning.

Published by AV² by Weigl
350 5th Avenue, 59th Floor
New York, NY 10118
Website: www.av2books.com    www.weigl.com

Library of Congress Cataloging-in-Publication Data

Kopp, Megan.
 Black widow spiders / Megan Kopp.
   p. cm. -- (Backyard animals)
 Includes index.
 ISBN 978-1-61690-622-1 (hardcover : alk. paper) -- ISBN 978-1-61690-628-3 (softcover : alk. paper)
 1. Black widow spider--Juvenile literature.  I. Title.

 QL458.42.T54K67 2011
 595.4'4--dc22

                         2010045059

Printed in the United States of America in North Mankato, Minnesota
1 2 3 4 5 6 7 8 9 0  15 14 13 12 11

052011
WEP37500

**Editor** Aaron Carr    **Design** Terry Paulhus

Every reasonable effort has been made to trace ownership and to obtain permission to reprint copyright material. The publishers would be pleased to have any errors or omissions brought to their attention so that they may be corrected in subsequent printings.

**Photo Credits**
Weigl acknowledges Getty Images and Dreamstime as photo suppliers for this title. Page 7, bottom right: copyright Todd Gearheart of Tarantulaspiders.com.

# Contents

# Meet the Black Widow

Black widows are a type of spider. They live in most parts of the world. Most black widow spiders live in areas that are warm and dry. They are usually found in dark, quiet places.

The black widow usually has a dark black body with a bright red or orange mark on its **abdomen**. This mark is shaped like an hourglass. For this reason, black widows are sometimes called hourglass spiders.

Most black widows found in nature are female. This is because males often die after mating. Sometimes, the female black widow eats the male. Adult female black widows have **venom**. All males and young black widows are harmless.

Black widow spiders can be found on every continent except Antarctica.

The adult female black widow has the strongest venom of all spiders in North America.

# All about Black Widows

Female black widows are about 1 inch (2.5 centimeters) in length. Males are less than half this size. Males and females also have different coloring. Only females have the black body and red marking that black widows are known for. Many male black widows are brown or gray in color. They sometimes have white and red stripes on their abdomen. Some males also have the hourglass marking. For males, the hourglass is often yellow or white.

There are five **species** of black widow in North America. The most common is the southern black widow. This black widow is found mainly in the southern United States. The least common species is the red widow. It is only found in parts of Florida. The red widow is a **threatened** species.

Most female black widows are about the same length as a paper clip.

# Types of Black Widow Spiders

## Southern, or Common, Black Widow

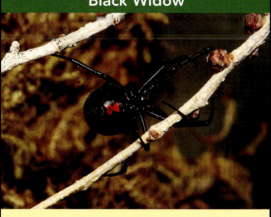

- Found across southern and eastern United States and Mexico
- Usually has a red hourglass marking

## Brown Widow

- Found in southern United States, Australia, and Africa
- Usually brown in color, but they can sometimes be gray

## Northern Black Widow

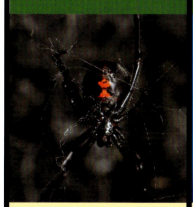

- Found in Canada and the northern United States
- Often has a row of red circle markings

## Western Black Widow

- Found in western parts of North America
- Often has an hourglass marking with one side larger than the other

## Red Widow

- Found only in Florida
- Usually has a reddish-orange upper body and a black abdomen

# Black Widow History

Spider **fossils** have been found that are more than 380 million years old. Many scientists believe spiders were among the first living things to live on land.

The history of spiders is difficult to study. This is because spider fossils are rare. Spiders have soft bodies with no bones. These bodies are not well-suited to forming fossils. A few ancient spiders have been preserved in **amber**. Other spiders have left marks in soft rock. Scientists use this information to learn about the history of spiders.

Scientists have found spiders preserved in amber that are more than 100 million years old.

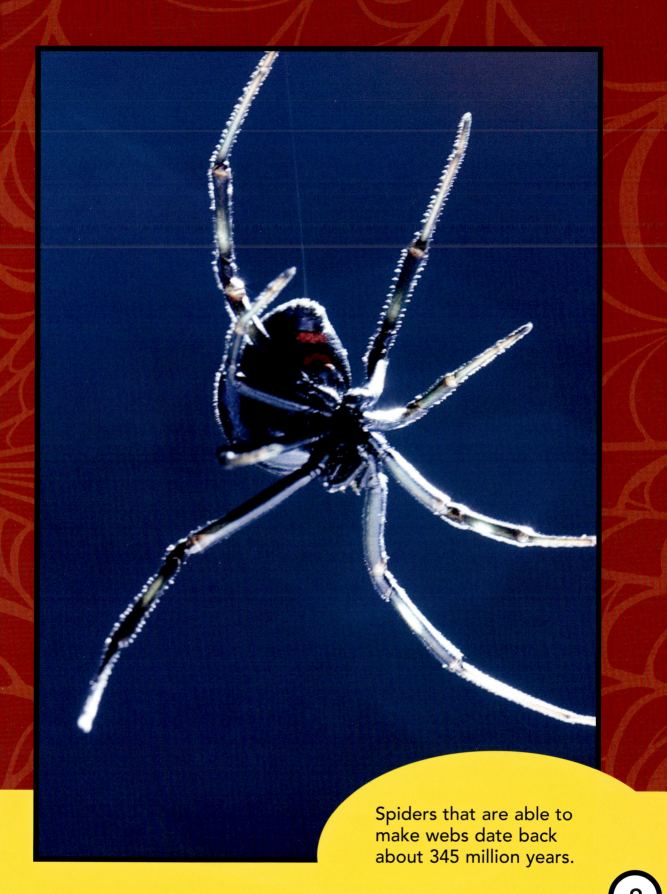

Spiders that are able to
make webs date back
about 345 million years.

# Black Widow Shelter

Black widows build their webs in wood piles, near holes, or in bushes close to the ground. Black widows can also be found in the basements and crawl spaces of houses.

Black widows live alone in their webs. They make their webs with **silk**. Black widows make silk in their bodies. Then, they use their legs to make the strands of silk into a web. Black widows cover their webs in a liquid that makes the web sticky. They use the sticky web to protect against **predators** and to capture **prey**.

Black widows can even use their webs to communicate with other spiders. Male black widows will vibrate a female's web to let her know he is there.

Black widow spider silk is the strongest of all spider silk.

Black widows make large webs that look messy.

# Black Widow Features

Black widows are **arachnids**. This group includes all spiders, scorpions, mites, and ticks. Arachnids have eight legs and two-part bodies. These bodies have hard outer shells called exoskeletons.

**SPINNERETS**
Small organs called **spinnerets** are found on the back of the abdomen. These organs make the silk that spiders use to build their webs.

**BODY**
All female black widows have dark, shiny black bodies. There are two main body parts. One part is the combined head and **thorax**. The other is the large, round abdomen.

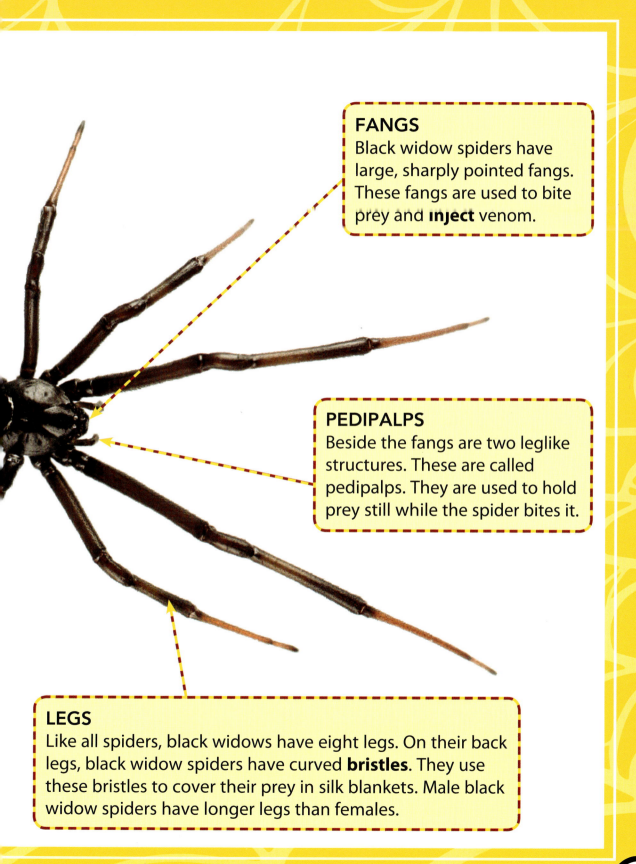

## FANGS

Black widow spiders have large, sharply pointed fangs. These fangs are used to bite prey and **inject** venom.

## PEDIPALPS

Beside the fangs are two leglike structures. These are called pedipalps. They are used to hold prey still while the spider bites it.

## LEGS

Like all spiders, black widows have eight legs. On their back legs, black widow spiders have curved **bristles**. They use these bristles to cover their prey in silk blankets. Male black widow spiders have longer legs than females.

# What Do Black Widows Eat?

Like most spiders, black widows eat insects. They do not hunt for food. Instead, black widows hang from their webs and wait for prey to come to them. They wrap their prey in a blanket of silk. Black widows capture flies, mosquitoes, caterpillars, beetles, and even large grasshoppers.

When the black widow is ready to eat, it covers its prey with a liquid that helps break it down. The black widow's prey will slowly turn into a liquid. Then, the black widow sticks its fangs into its prey and sucks out the contents.

If a beetle avoids being eaten by a black widow or other predator, it will usually live about one year.

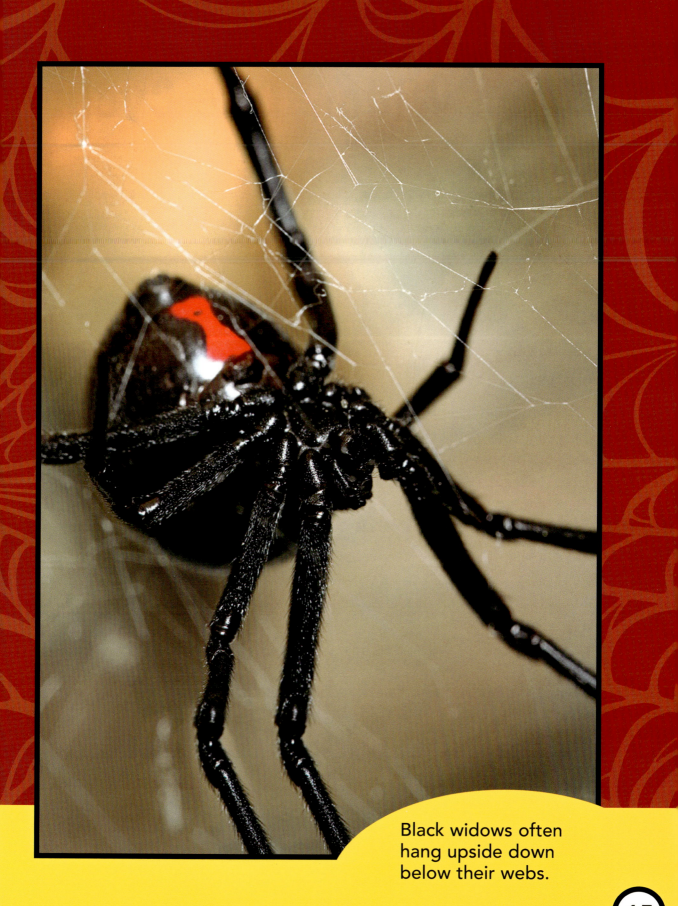

Black widows often hang upside down below their webs.

# Black Widow Life Cycle

Female black widows lay egg sacs during the summer. These sacs can contain up to 750 eggs. Hundreds of spiderlings are born, but only a small number survive into adulthood.

## Birth

The female black widow covers her egg sacs in silk to hide them from other insects and animals. She then guards the egg sacs until the young spiders hatch. This usually takes about 30 days.

## One Day to One Month

Spiderlings are orange and white. They are small enough to pass through an opening less than 0.04 inches (1 millimeter) wide. Spiderlings spin a silk web. When the wind catches this web, it lifts the spiderlings off to a new home. This process is called ballooning.

Most of the spiderlings die from lack of food and shelter. Others are eaten by larger spiders. Black widows are usually full grown after two to four months.

## One to Three Months

As black widows grow, their exoskeletons become too small. They **molt** to shed their exoskeleton. Black widows become black in color as they age.

## Adult

Female black widow spiders molt up to nine times as they grow to adults. Females have been known to live as long as three years. Male black widows only live for one or two months.

# Encountering Black Widows

Black widows are not aggressive. Still, they will bite if they feel they are in danger. For this reason, it is best to keep away from black widows and their webs.

Most black widow encounters happen when people are not expecting it. To avoid surprising a black widow, it is best to use caution in dark, quiet areas. Wear gloves when handling wood from a wood pile. Also, check behind boxes and other items stored in basements and garages before picking them up. Black widow bites should be treated by a doctor right away.

## Fascinating Facts

Black widows are nocturnal. This means they are active at night and sleep during the day.

Only female black widows bite people.

# Myths and Legends

The name *arachnid* comes from a Greek story about a weaver named Arachne. In Greek myth, Athena was the goddess of war and handicrafts. Athena was jealous of Arachne's talent and beauty. She turned Arachne into a spider.

Spiders are a common figure in many American Indian stories. In most stories, the spider is a wise female. Spiders are often a symbol of creativity and patience.

Navajo legends tell how Spider Woman taught Navajo women to weave.

# A Strong Symbol

*This Osage legend is about how the spider came to be a symbol of the Osage people.*

Long ago, the Osage people were separated into groups. Each group found an animal that would become its teacher.

One day, a chief was walking through the forest. He came across deer tracks and became very excited. He thought the deer could be the symbol of his group. He followed the tracks. He ran faster and faster until he ran into a spider's web.

The spider asked why the chief was running so fast. The chief said he was seeking a symbol for his people. The spider said she could be a symbol for the chief's people. The chief was not sure. He thought spiders were weak. The spider explained that she builds a web and lets everything she needs come to her. She offered to teach the chief how his people could do the same. This is how the spider became a symbol of the Osage people.

# Frequently Asked Questions

## Do all female black widows eat males after mating?

**Answer:** No. Most males live to mate again and later die on their own. Females only eat the males on rare occasions. However, the female Australian redback spider is known to eat the male more often.

## Will a person die from a black widow bite?

**Answer:** Not likely. Black widow spider bites are painful, and they can cause illness. However, people rarely die from a black widow bite.

## How venomous are black widows?

**Answer:** The venom of a black widow spider is 15 times stronger than that of a rattlesnake. However, black widows are so small, they cannot inject enough of this powerful venom to cause serious harm to large animals or people.

# Words to Know

**abdomen:** the back segment of a spider

**amber:** hardened tree sap

**arachnids:** a class of animals without backbones that includes spiders, ticks, mites, and scorpions

**bristles:** coarse, stiff hairs

**fossils:** ancient remains of animals and plants

**inject:** to force a fluid into a body

**molt:** to cast off, or shed, the outer surface in order to allow new growth

**predators:** animals that hunt other animals for food

**prey:** animals that are hunted by other animals for food

**silk:** the material spiders make in their bodies and use to build webs

**species:** a group of animals with the same characteristics

**spinnerets:** the parts of a spider's body that makes silk

**thorax:** the portion of the body between the head and the abdomen

**threatened:** any species of plant or animal that could become endangered in the near future

**venom:** a type of poison

# Index

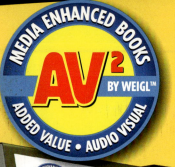

# Log on to www.av2books.com

AV² by Weigl brings you media enhanced books that support active learning. Go to www.av2books.com, and enter the special code found on page 2 of this book. You will gain access to enriched and enhanced content that supplements and complements this book. Content includes video, audio, web links, quizzes, a slide show, and activities.

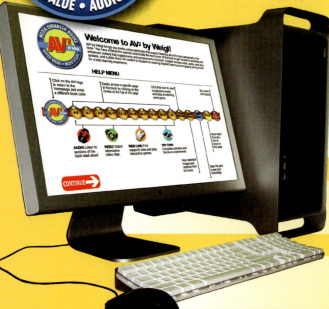

## Audio
Listen to sections of the book read aloud.

## Video
Watch informative video clips.

## Embedded Weblinks
Gain additional information for research.

## Try This!
Complete activities and hands-on experiments.

# WHAT'S ONLINE?

|  Try This! |  Embedded Weblinks |  Video | EXTRA FEATURES |
|---|---|---|---|
| Identify different types of black widow spiders.<br><br>List important features of the black widow spider.<br><br>Compare the similarities and differences between young and adult black widows.<br><br>Test your knowledge of black widow spiders. | Learn more about black widow spider identification.<br><br>Find out more information on the history of black widow spiders.<br><br>Complete an interactive activity.<br><br>Learn more about what to do when encountering black widow spiders.<br><br>Read more stories and legends about black widow spiders. | Watch a video about black widow spider behavior.<br><br>See a black widow spider in its natural environment. |  **Audio** Listen to sections of the book read aloud.<br><br> **Key Words** Study vocabulary, and complete a matching word activity.<br><br> **Slide Show** View images and captions, and prepare a presentation.<br><br> **Quizzes** Test your knowledge. |

**AV² was built to bridge the gap between print and digital. We encourage you to tell us what you like and what you want to see in the future.**

## Sign up to be an AV² Ambassador at www.av2books.com/ambassador.